First edition published 2016 by Books Beyond Words.

Text & illustrations © Books Beyond Words 2016.

ISBN 978-1-78458-080-3

British Library Cataloguing-in-Publication Data
A catalogue record for this book is available from the British Library.

Printed by Book Printing UK, Peterborough.

Books Beyond Words is a Community Interest Company registered in England and Wales (7557861).

St George's Hospital Charity is a registered charity (no. 241527).

Contents

Storyline

The following words are provided for readers and supporters who want some ideas about one possible story. Most readers make their own story up from the pictures.

1. Ellie and Rob come out of the sea. It's too cold and windy for swimming.

2. They find their friends, Miles and Nadya. Nadya is building a sandcastle.

3. The sun comes out. Nadya sees an ice cream van.

4. She joins the queue to buy an ice cream.

5. Oh no! Nadya trips on some seaweed and drops her ice cream. The lady in the ice cream van sees.

6. The ice cream lady is kind and gives Nadya a new ice cream.

7. Everyone relaxes on the beach. Miles pumps up a lilo.

8. Miles walks to the sea with the lilo. He's got his phone in his pocket.

9. Miles lies on the lilo in the sea. He uses his phone.

10. A seagull swoops down and pops the lilo! Miles is shocked. He drops his phone.

11. Miles is in trouble. Rob phones for help.

12. The lifeguard runs into the sea to rescue Miles.

13. Ellie and Nadya look after Miles and make sure he is ok. Rob says thank you to the lifeguard.

14. The friends have a barbecue on the beach.

15. Uh oh, the seagull is back. Is it going to cause more trouble?

Pictures to colour for yourself

You can bring your own artistic talents to the story and colour some of the pictures for yourself on the next pages.

Felt tips work best for colouring these pictures.

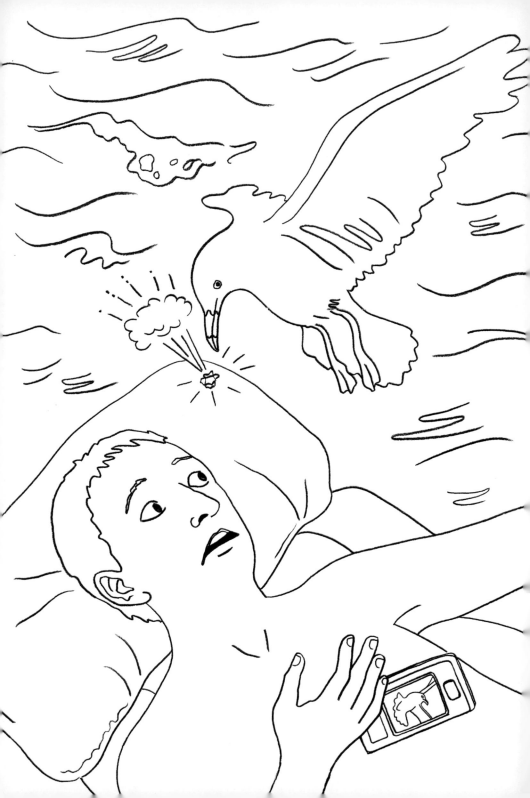

Picture This

Valuing individual creativity is very important to our sense of well-being. This idea was at the centre of everything we did in this project and helped bring out the best in all of us.

Kent libraries in partnership with Beyond Words worked with self-advocates and artists to develop three innovative picture books. The storylines were developed through a series of drama workshops with self-advocates engaging in a story making process. Using drama to improvise scenes and develop stories for the artists to capture, we created three original picture books for people with learning disabilities.

Beyond Words' project team made 15 visits to nine Kent book clubs, holding drama workshops to invent the original stories. The artists drew the first set of pictures based on the drama sessions, and self-advocates then read and commented on them. The pictures were edited and redrawn in response to the feedback from the book clubs and readers in local day centres and activity groups.

Trialling the pictures several times across multiple visits to book clubs helped the artists to make the stories as clear and engaging as possible. Honouring the opinions and choices of people on the project has kept the book club readers' voices genuinely at the centre of the stories.

There has been a lot of laughter on this project and people have told us how much they have enjoyed taking part.

Related titles

A Balloon Adventure (2016) by Dartford, Maidstone and Sittingbourne book clubs, illustrated by Gaby Weigert. Stuart and Zoe are going on holiday in their hot air balloon. A gust of wind catches them by surprise but with a bit of help the pair are soon back on track. Their trip ends up being a much bigger adventure than they had expected.

A Night in Space (2016) by Edenbridge, Tonbridge and Tunbridge Wells book clubs, illustrated by Beth Aulton. Annie loves outer space. One night, Annie dreams that she flies to another planet and meets a friendly alien and some space explorers. It's up to Annie and the alien to help the space explorers find what they are looking for.

Ginger is a Hero (2015) by Beth Webb. Mary and her neighbour Mrs Hill don't get on. Mrs Hill gets really cross when her cat, Ginger, makes friends with Mary. But when Mrs Hill collapses at home, it's down to Mary and Ginger to save her life.

Beyond Words

To find out more about Beyond Words training and publications please visit our website: www.booksbeyondwords.co.uk

Artist

Lucy Bergonzi is an artist and designer who has worked as a muralist, as a community artist, as a set designer and scenic artist in the theatre, and as a studio artist. She has worked for several years in the community and voluntary sector, and has wide experience of supporting people with learning disabilities. Lucy's website is www.lucybergonzi.co.uk.

Acknowledgments

A big thank you to the three book clubs who created the story. Dover Discovery book club: William, Julie, Mandy, Steve and supporters Sue and Lynne. Deal book club: Paul, Marc and Ian. Folkestone book club: Cas, Raymond, Diana, Julie, Jane, Lisa, Richard, Lee, Helen, Matthew, Ayden, Karen, Claire, Marie, Leanne, Alan and supporter Karen.

Thank you to the book clubs, groups and day services who trialled the pictures: Chatty Bunch Ashford, Ashford Community Day Services, Beyond Words Book Group Swanley (members are students from Milestone Academy), Skillnet Group, Deal Fishing Group, Margate Ready2Read Group.

We are grateful to Arts Council England for their generous funding of this project.

How to read this book

There is no right or wrong way to read this book. Remember it is not necessary to be able to read the words.

1. Some people are not used to reading books. Start at the beginning and read the story in each picture. Encourage the reader to hold the book themselves and to turn the pages at their own pace.

2. Whether you are reading the book with one person or with a group, encourage them to tell the story in their own words. You may think something different is happening in the pictures yourself, but that doesn't matter. Don't challenge the reader(s) or suggest their ideas are wrong.

3. You can help readers along by asking questions like:

- Who do you think that is?
- What is happening?
- How is he or she feeling?
- Do you ever feel like that?

4. You don't have to read the whole book in one sitting. Have fun with it: allow people time to chat about what they are reading and to follow the pictures at their own pace.

5. You can use the pictures as a storyboard for a drama group to create a play of the book.